This coloring book b

Kitchen & Cooking Coloring Book For Kids © 2021 by Creative Casita Publishing
All rights reserved. No part of this book may be used or reproduced in any manner whatsoever without written permission except in the case of brief quotations embodied in critical articles and reviews.
First Edition: 2021

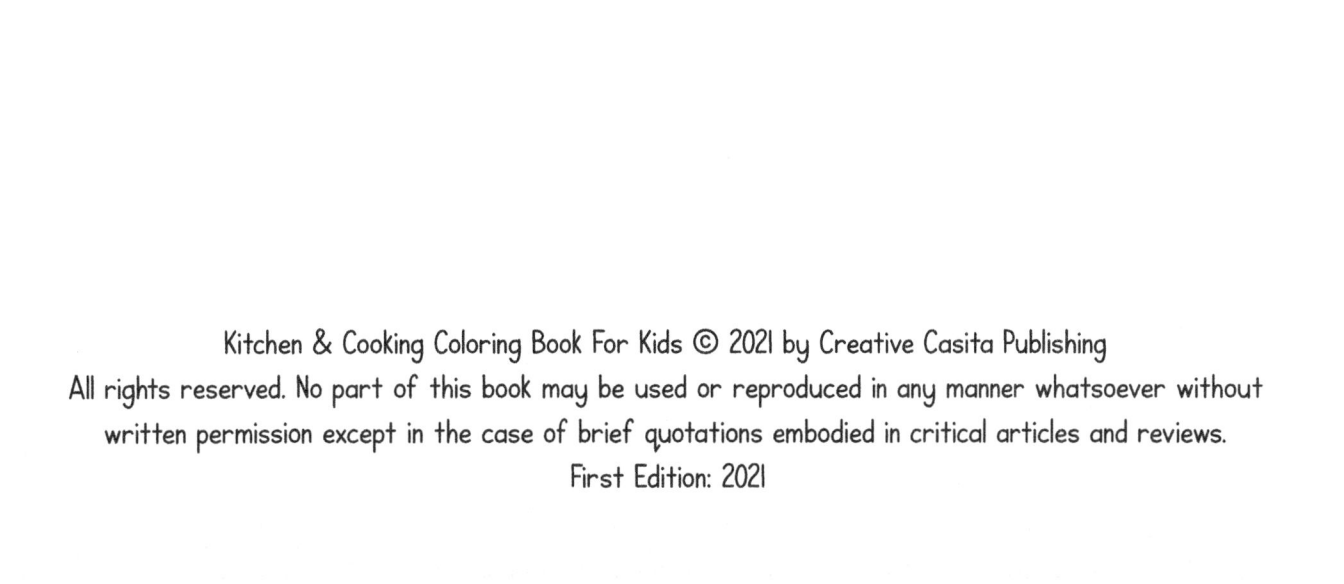

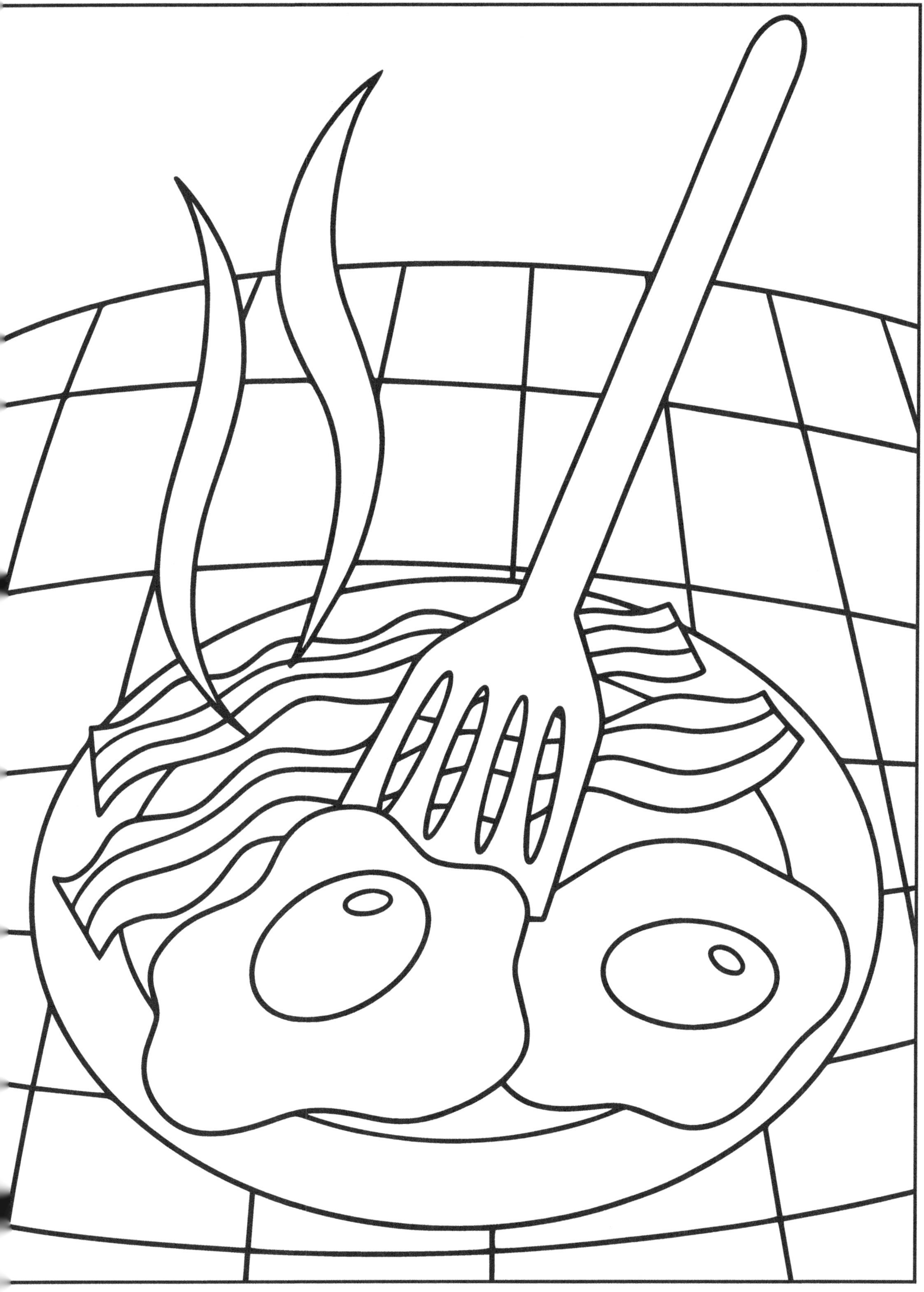

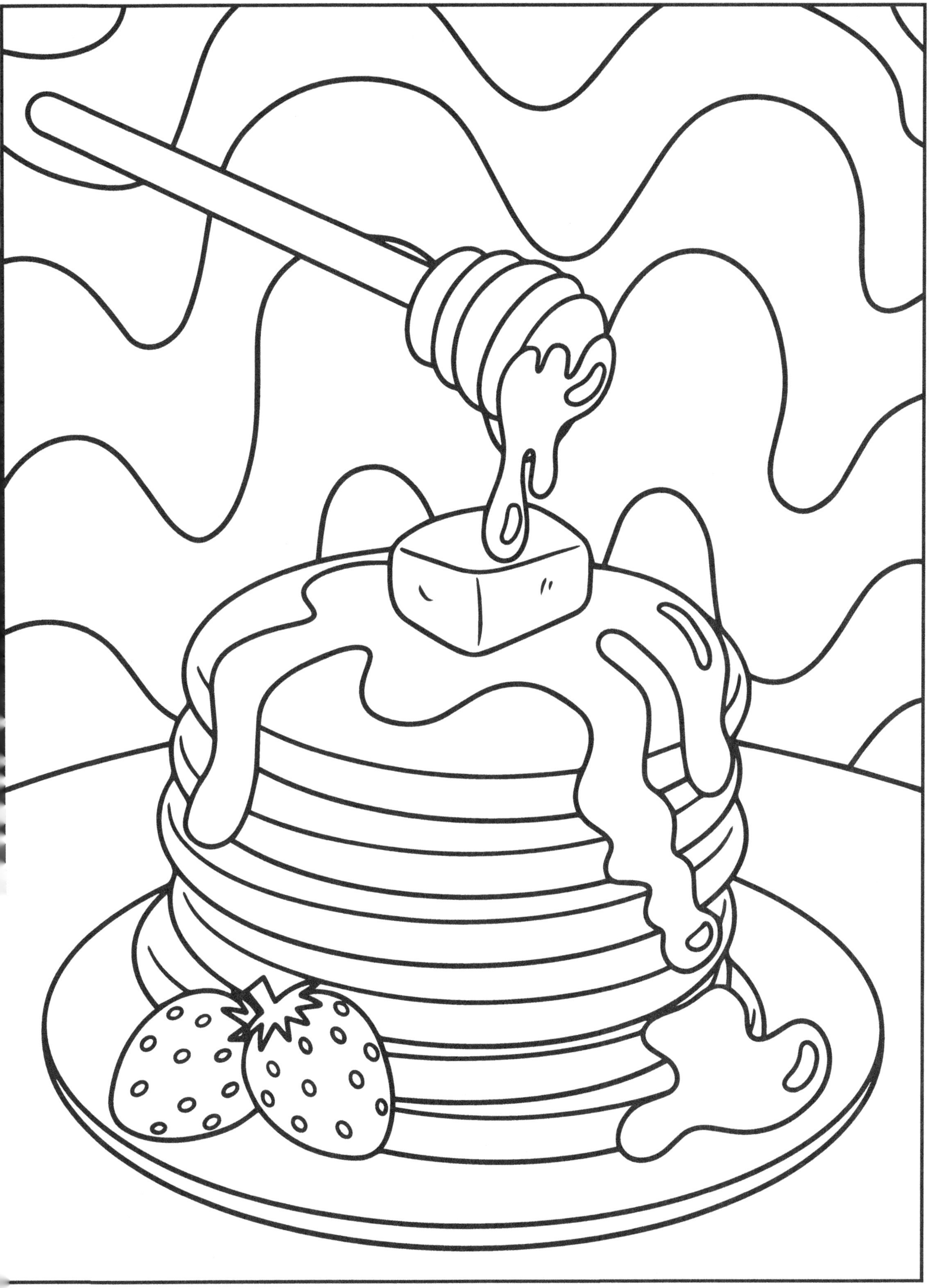

FLOUR

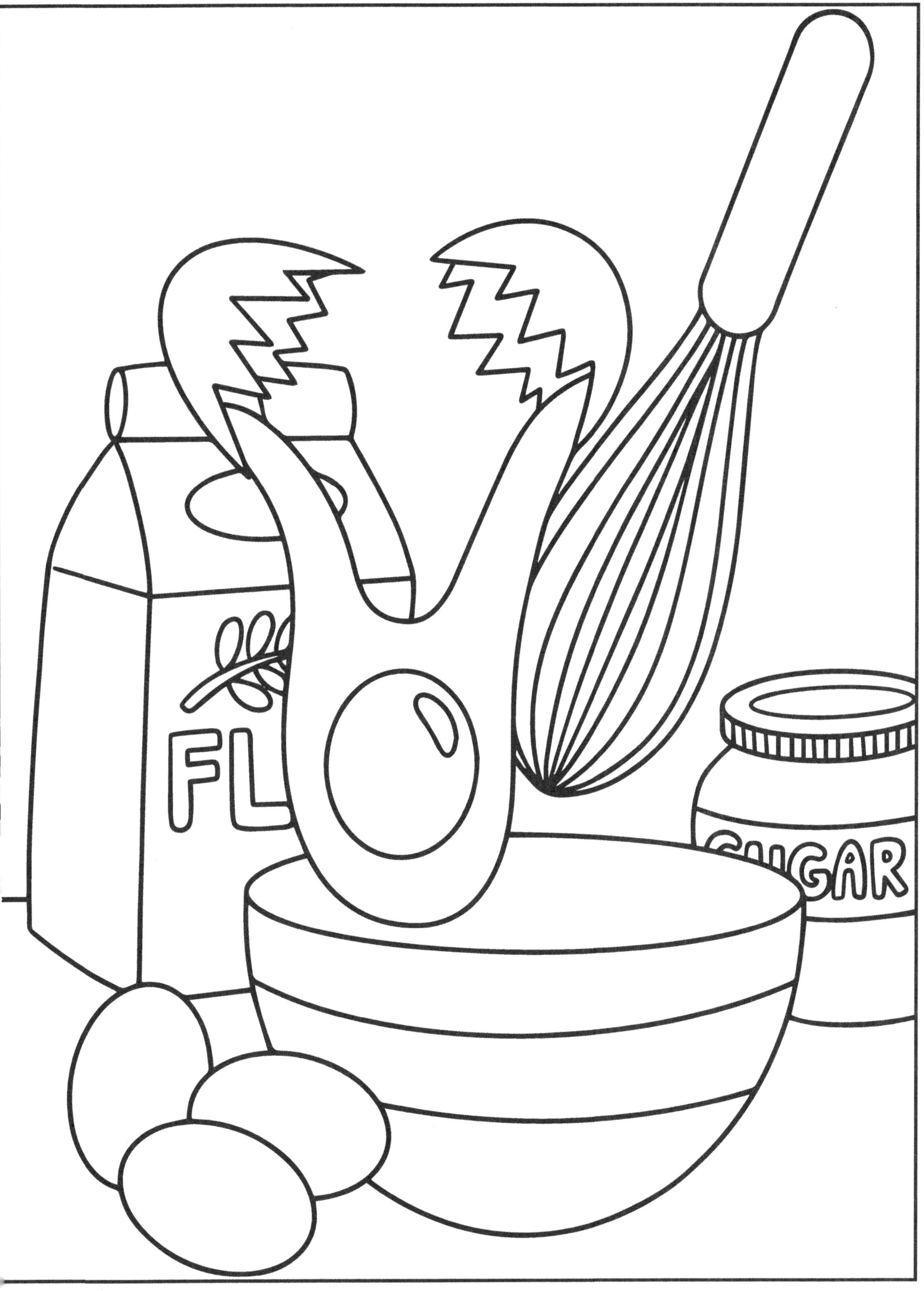
FL
UGAR

LET'S COOK

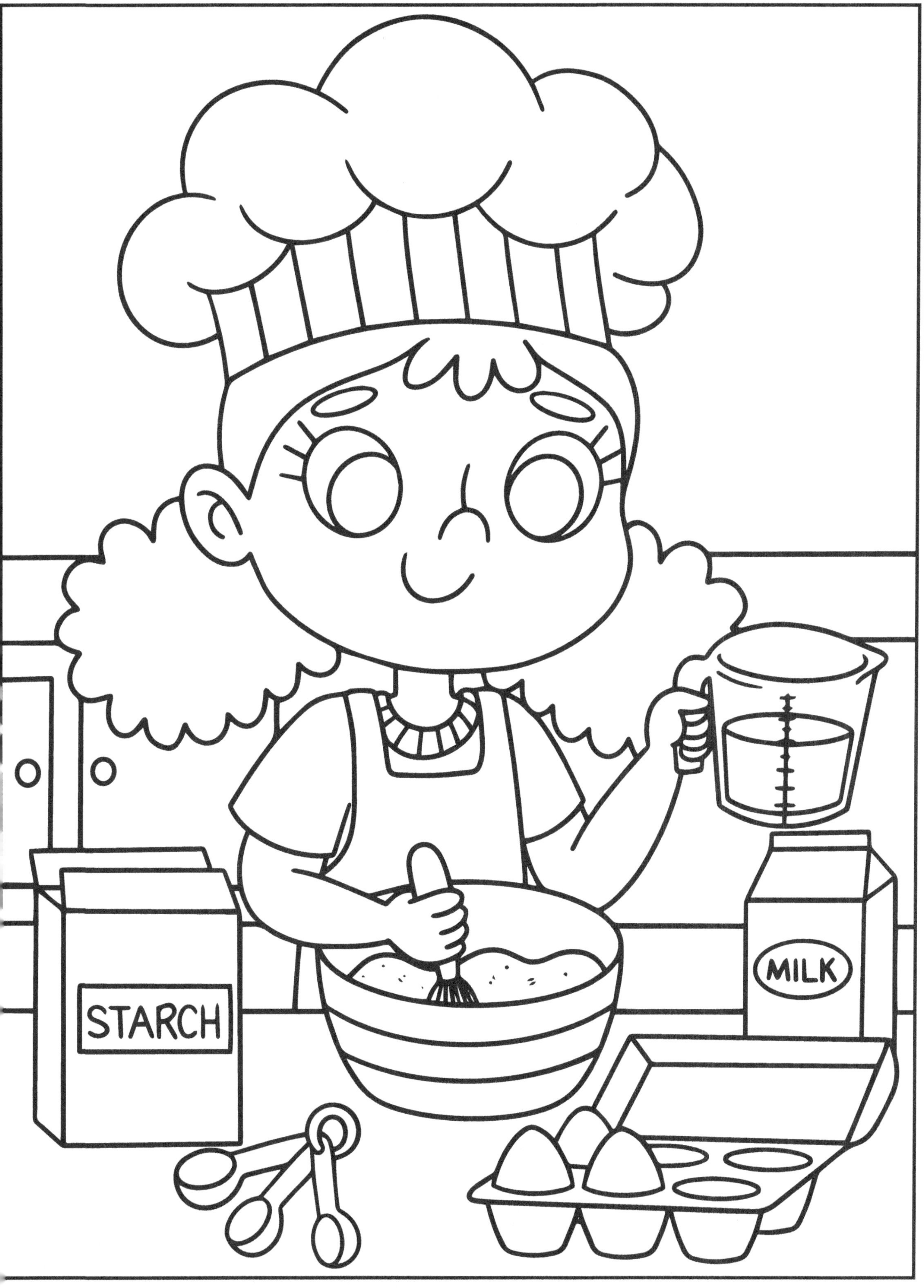
STARCH
MILK

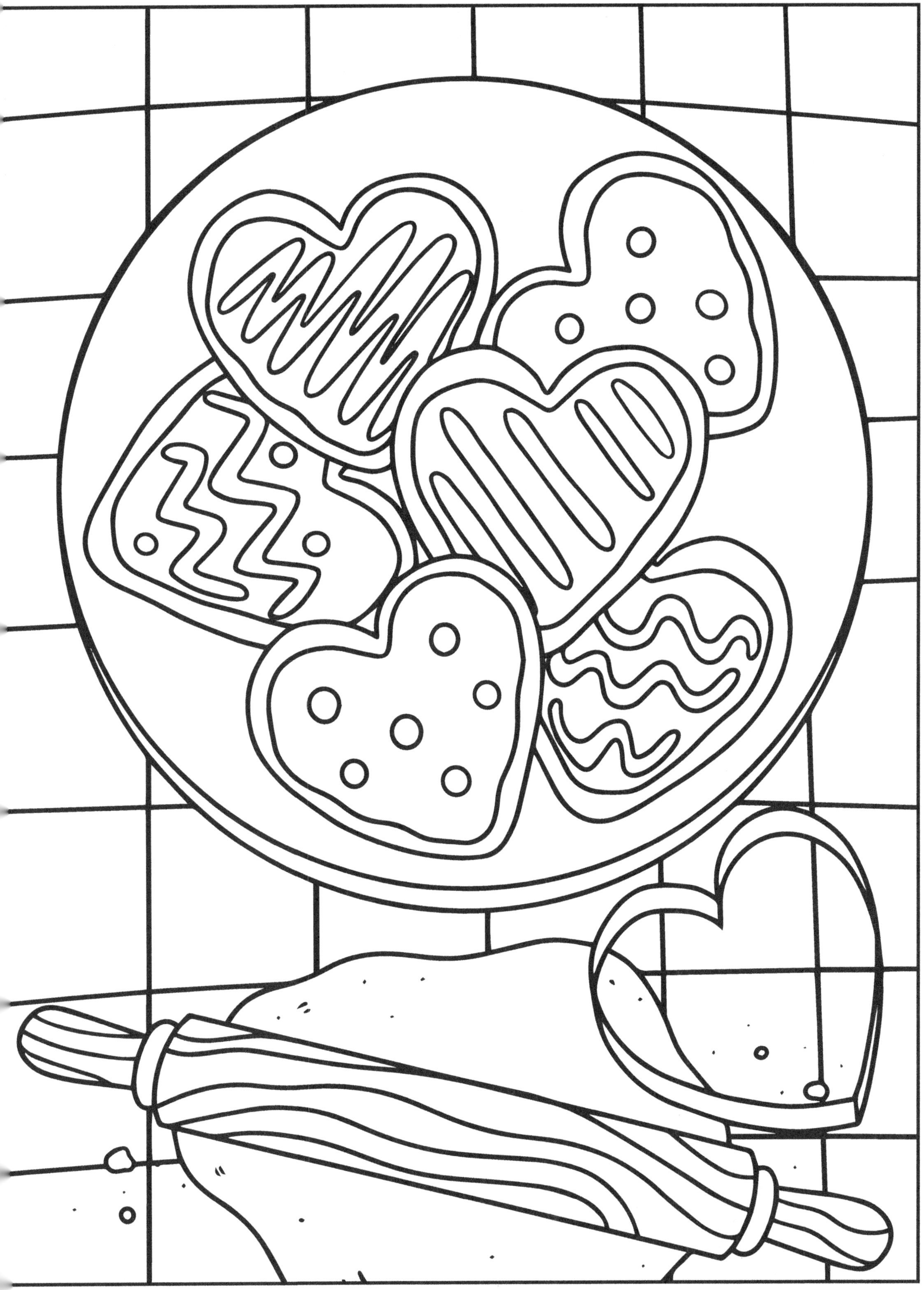

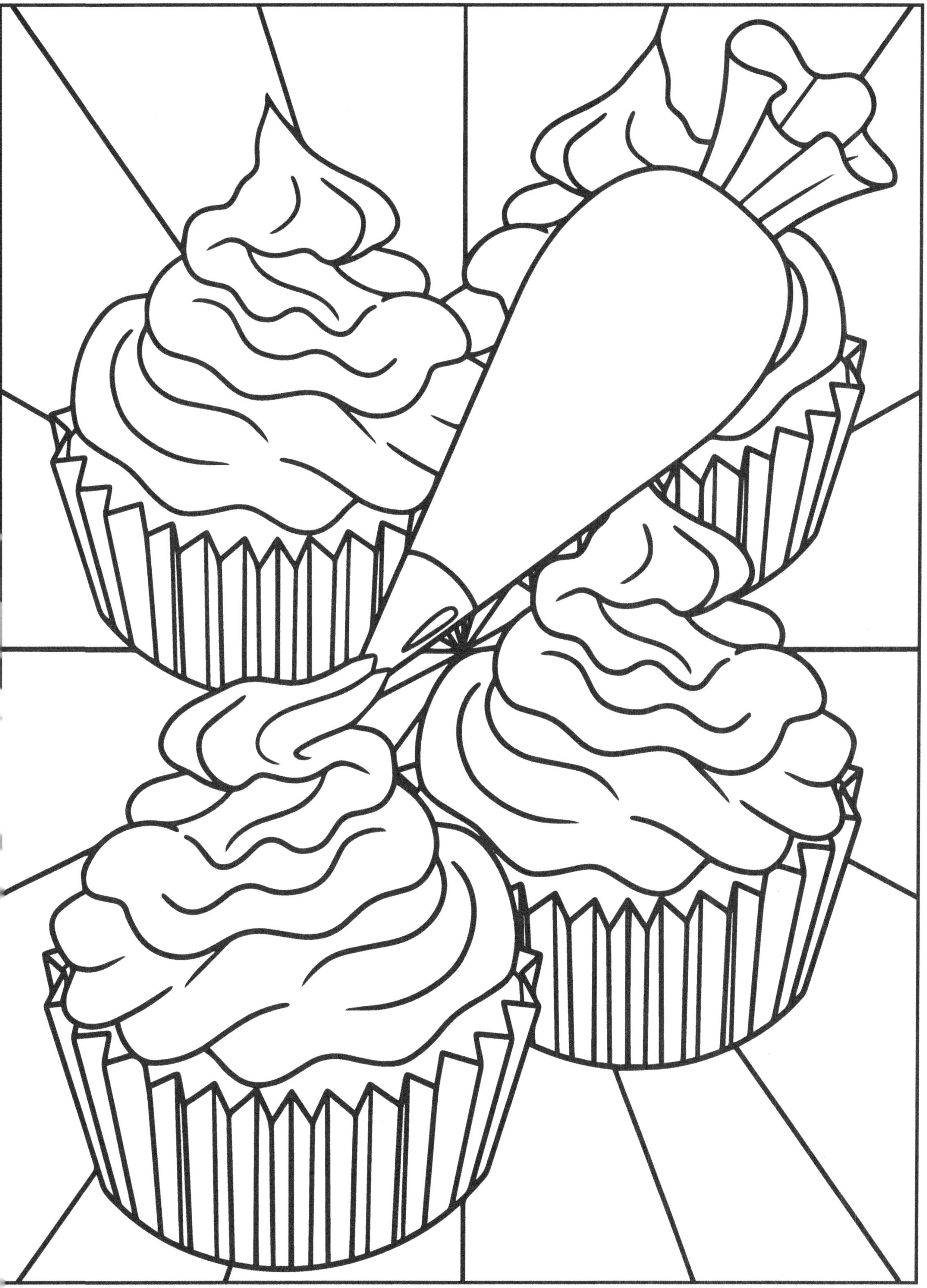

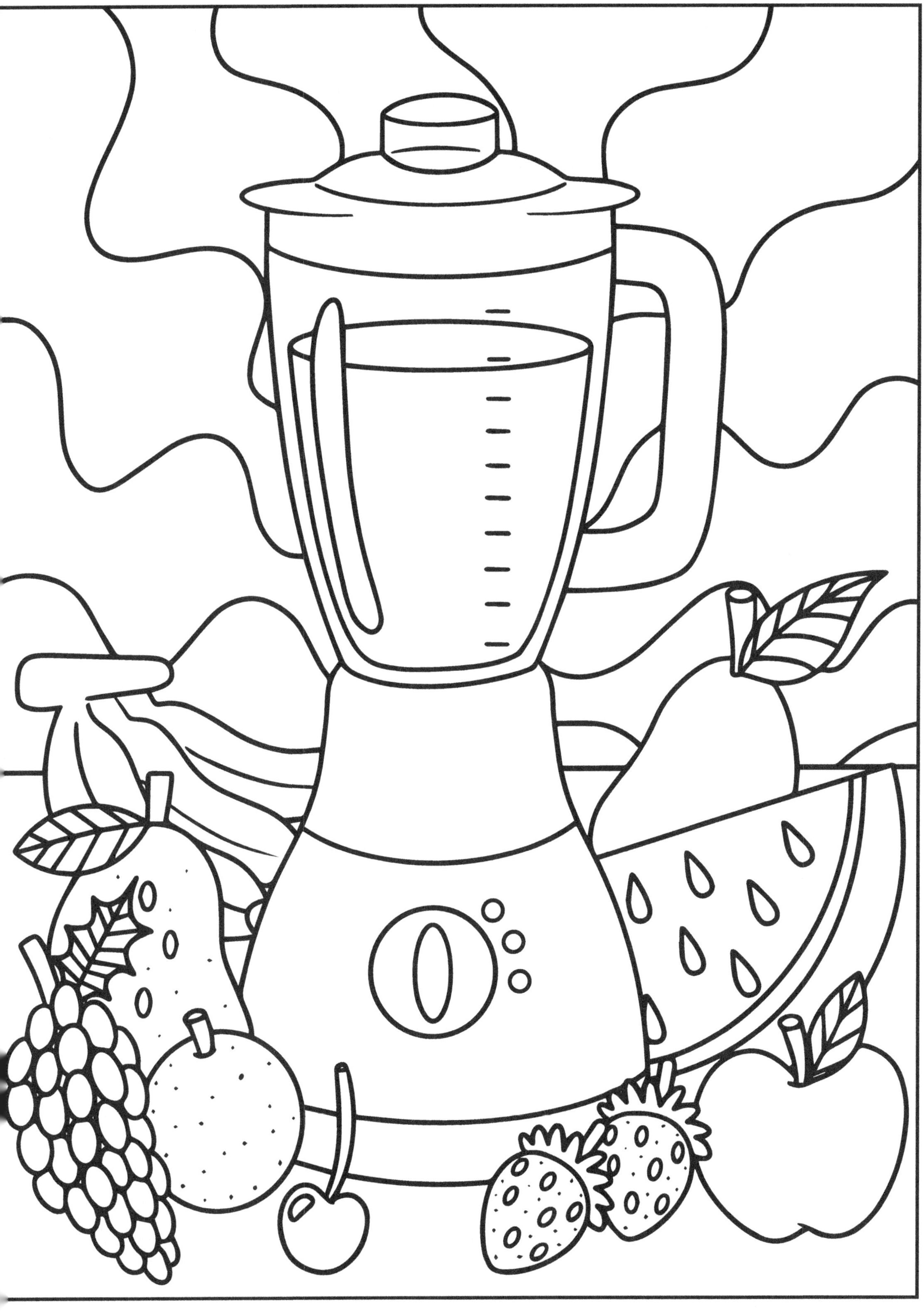

MIX IT UP!

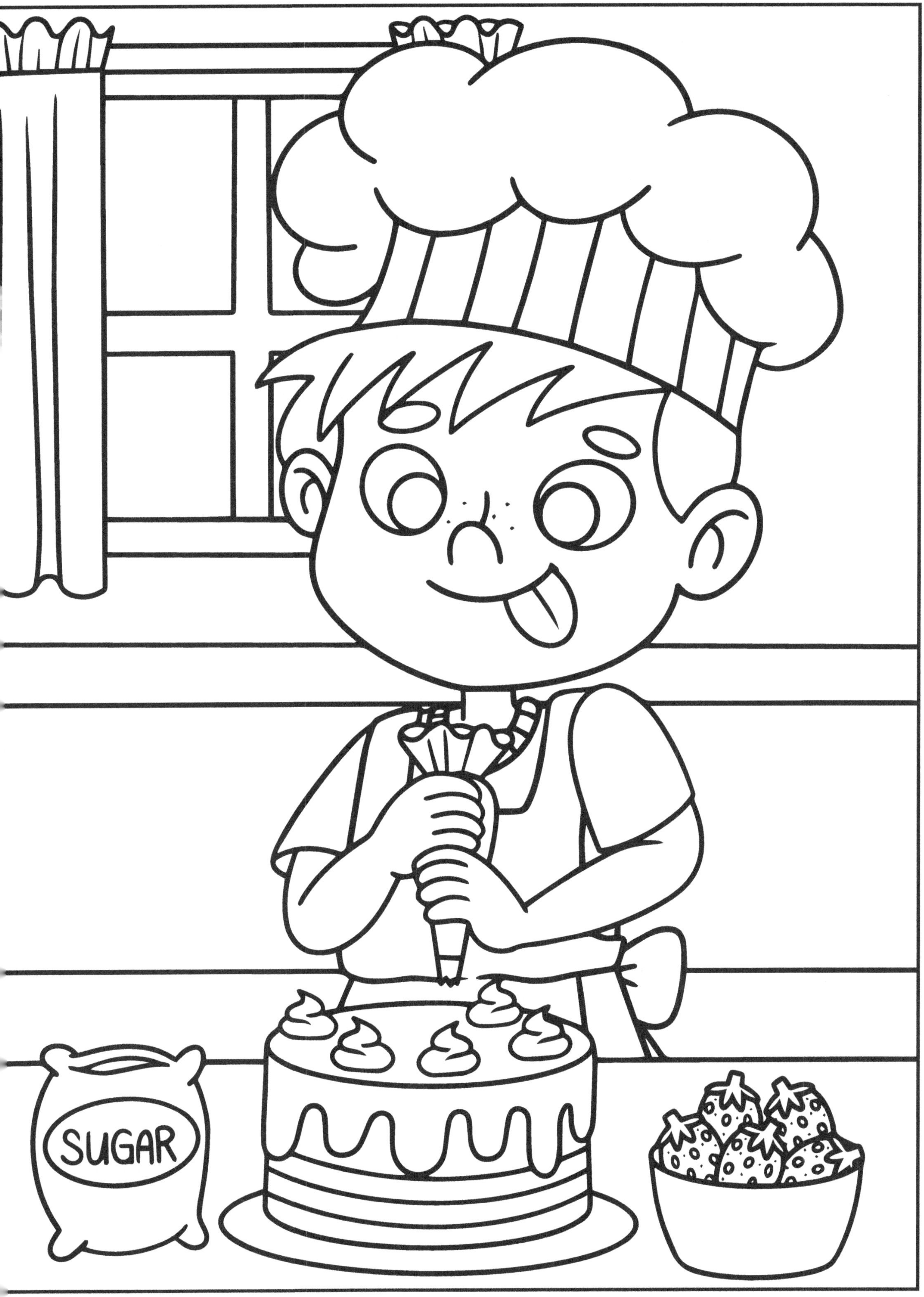
SUGAR

What's Cooking?

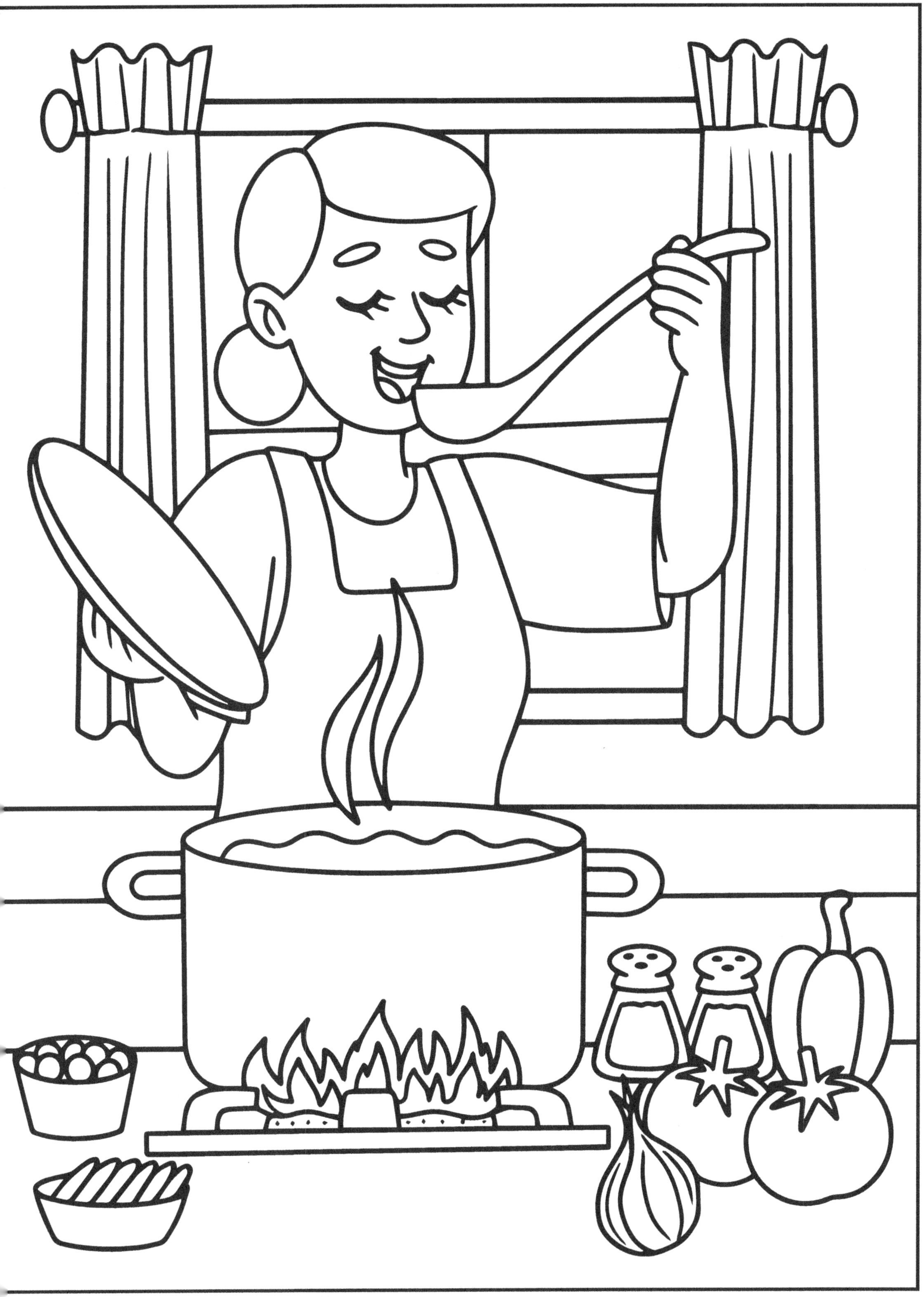

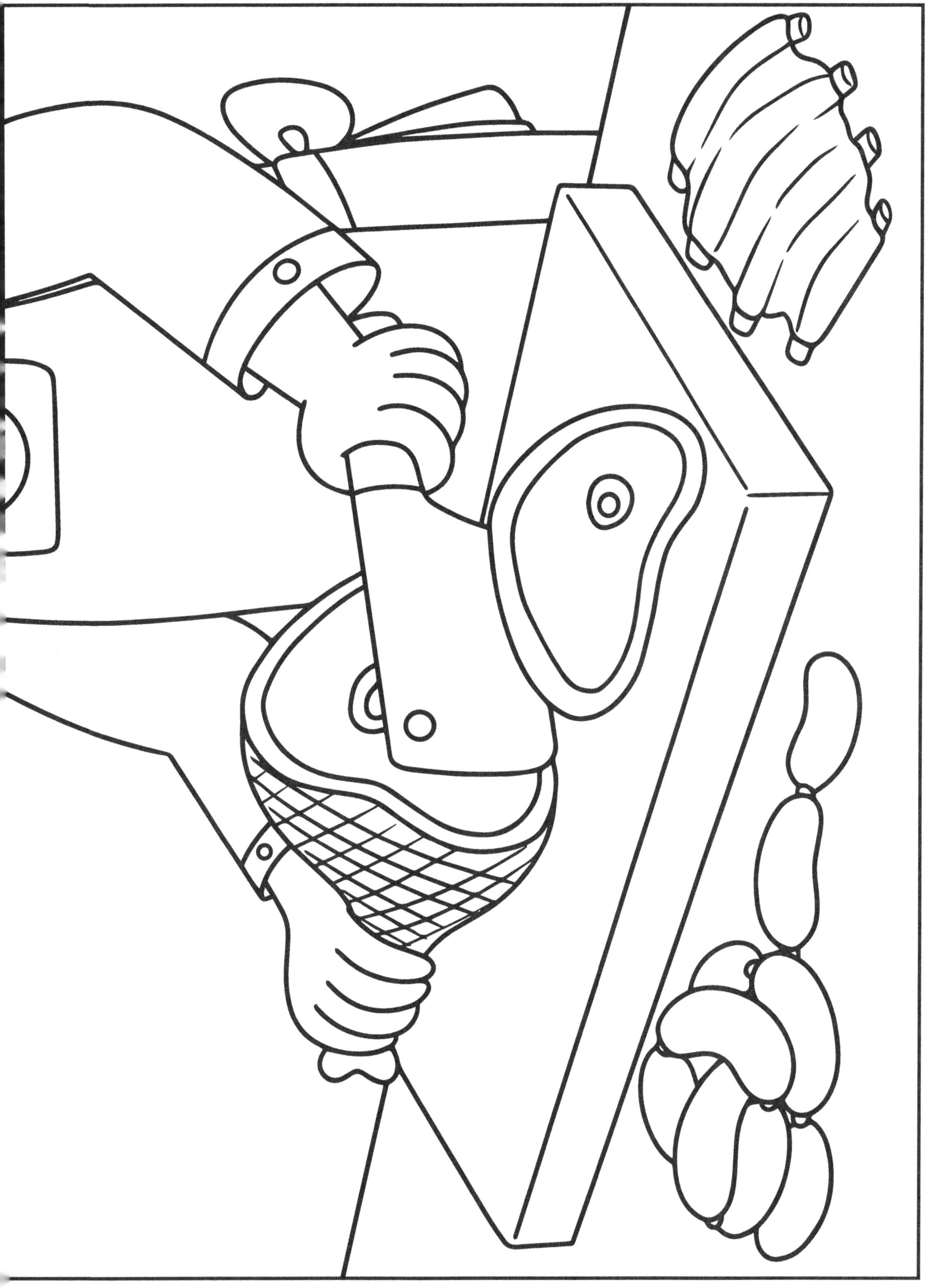

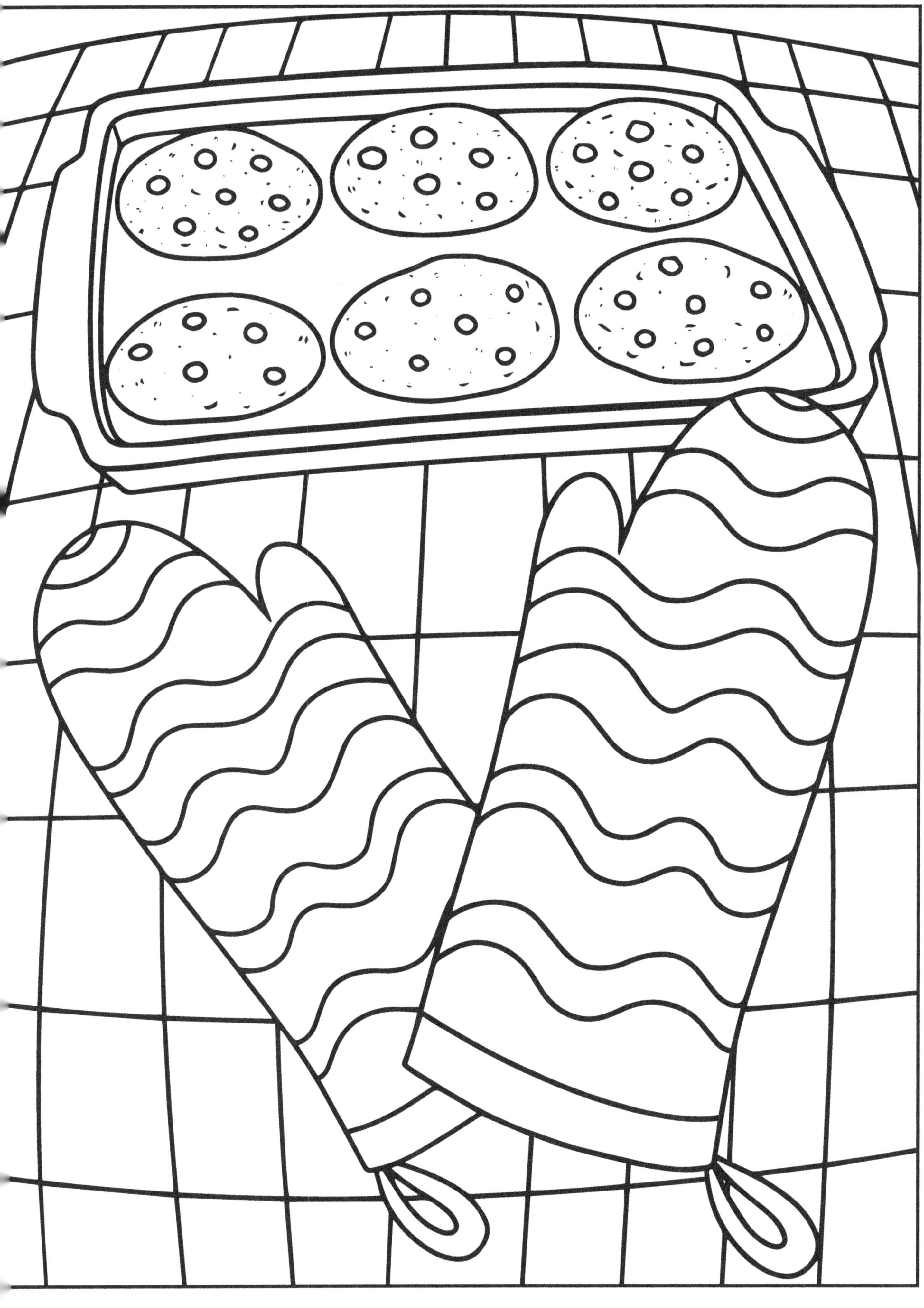

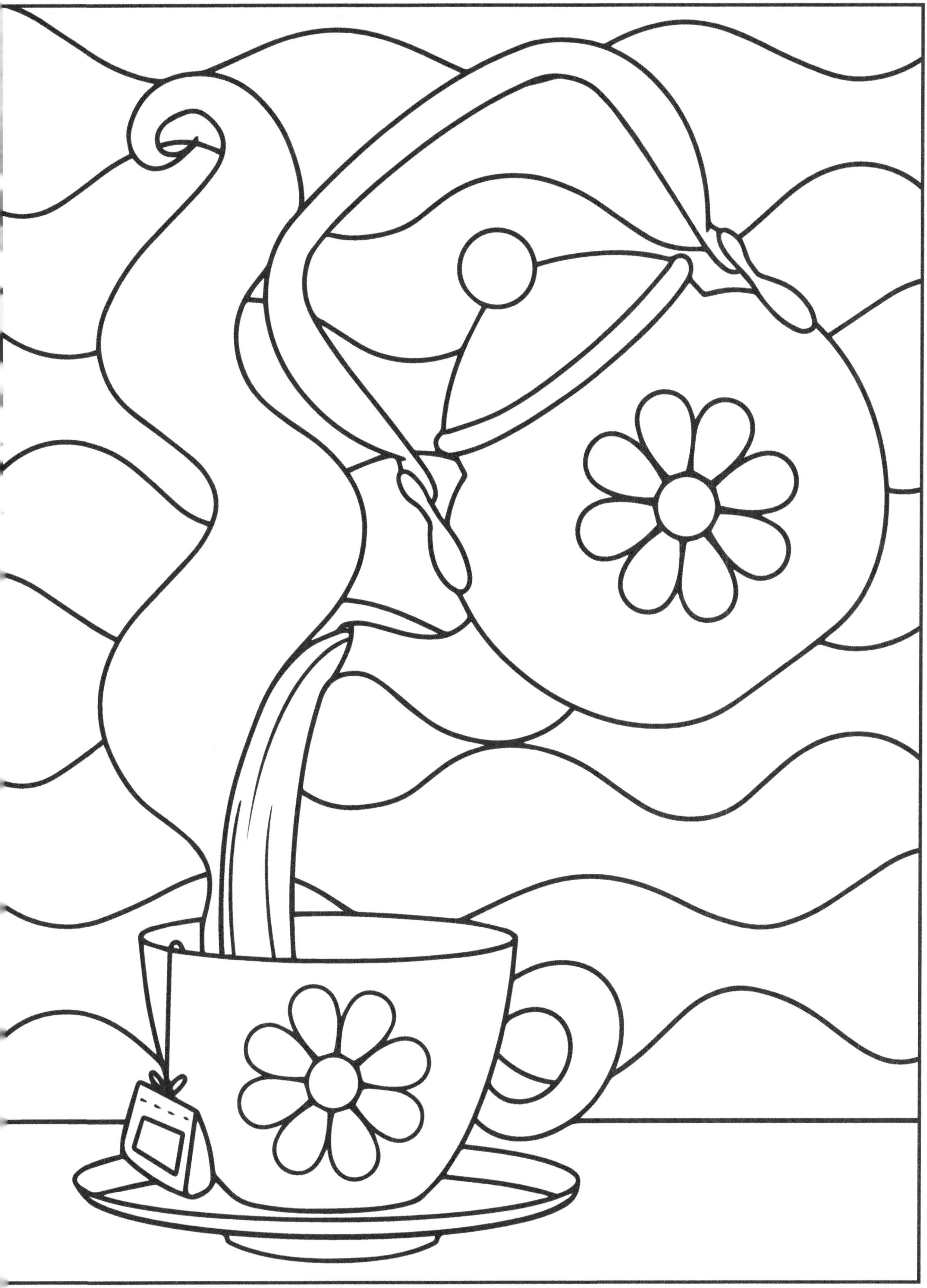

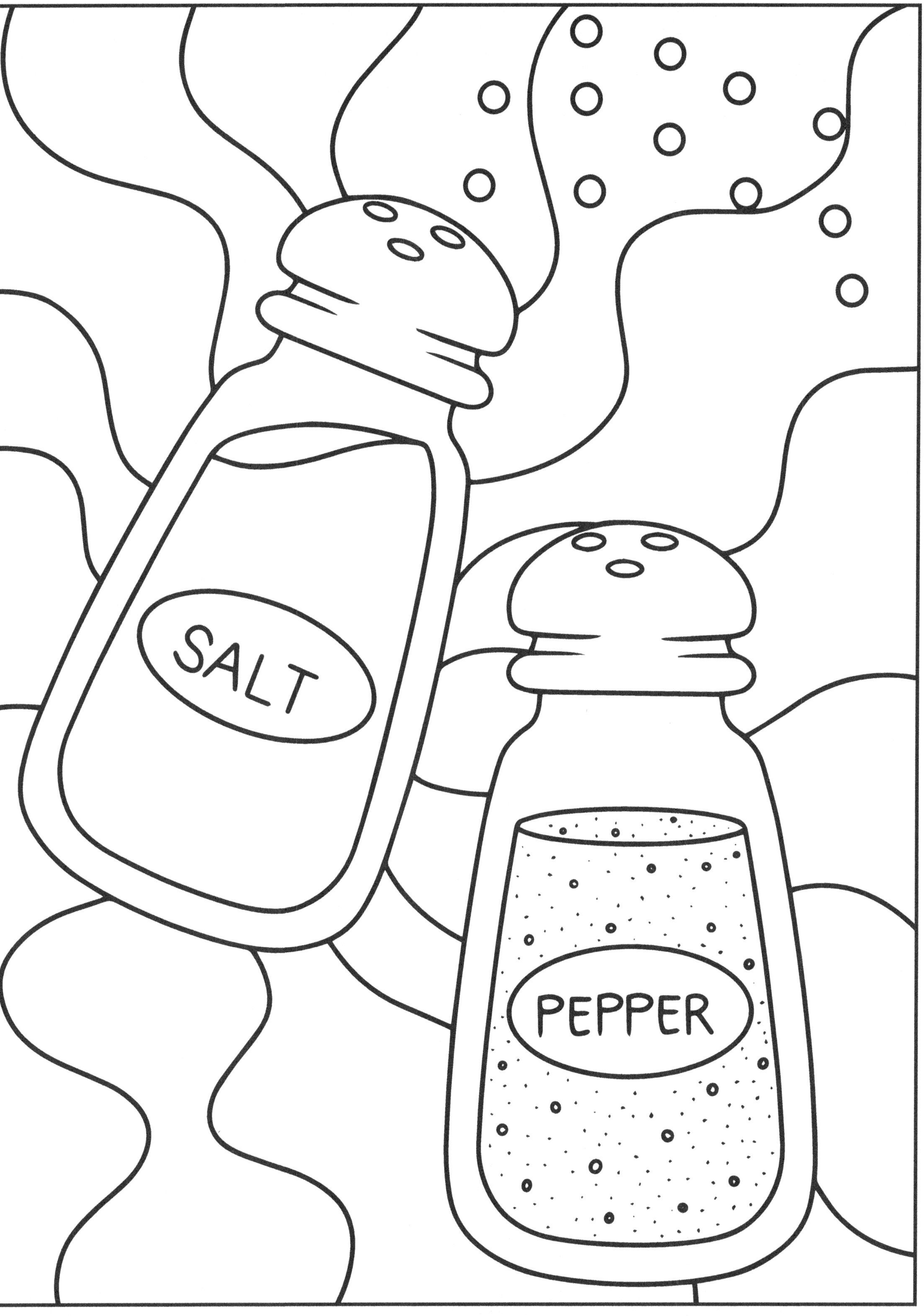
SALT
PEPPER

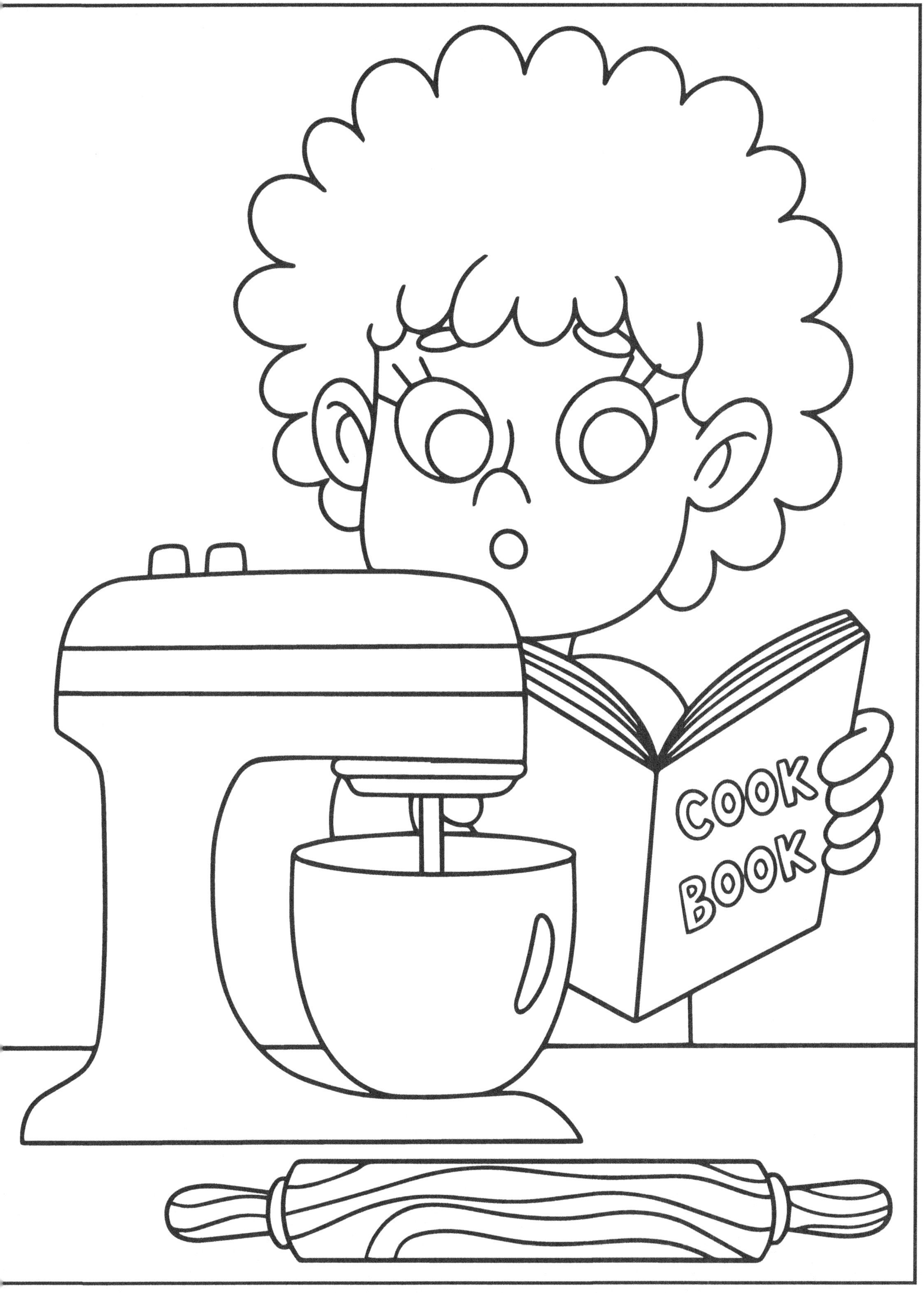
COOK
BOOK

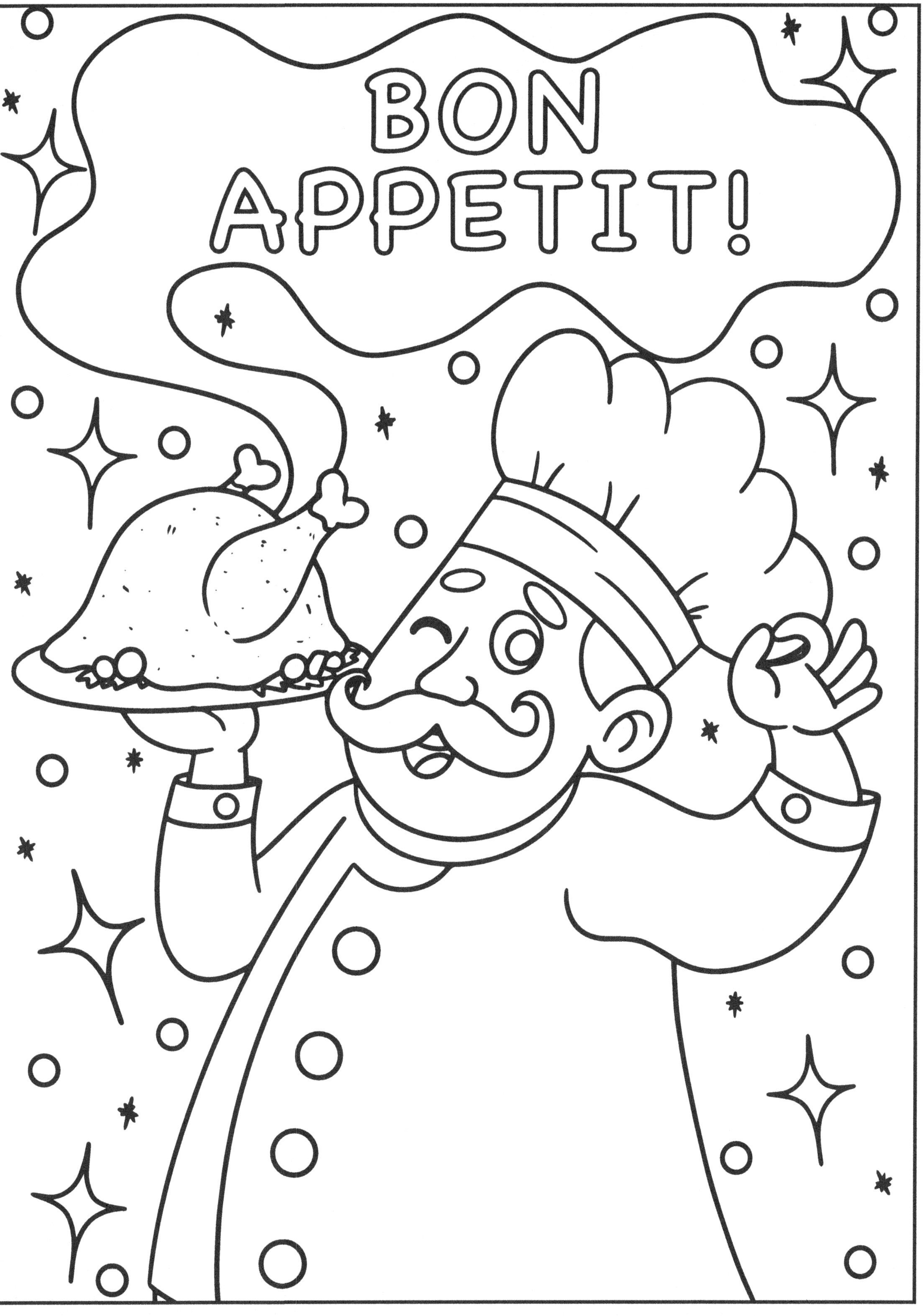
BON
APPETIT!

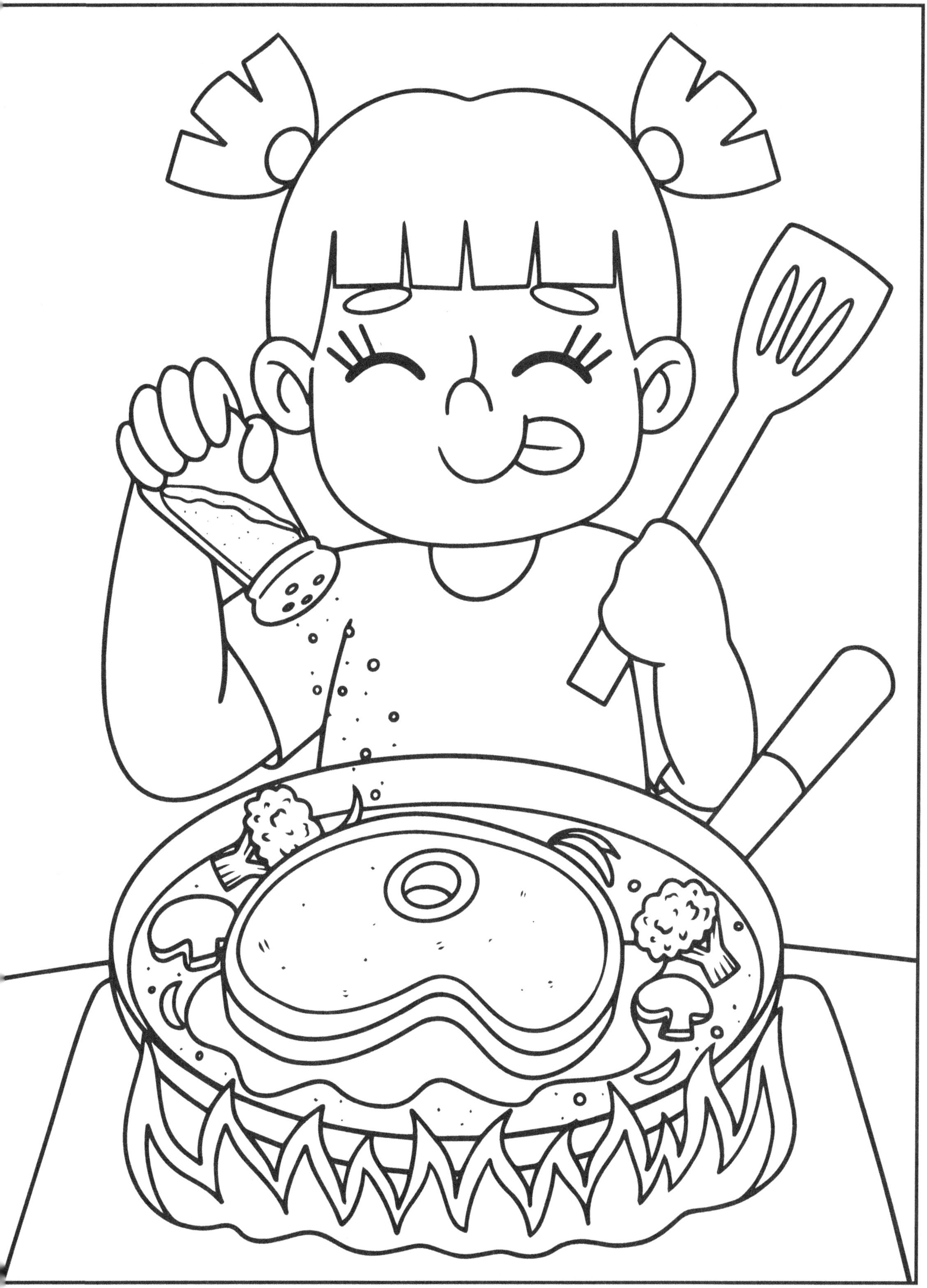

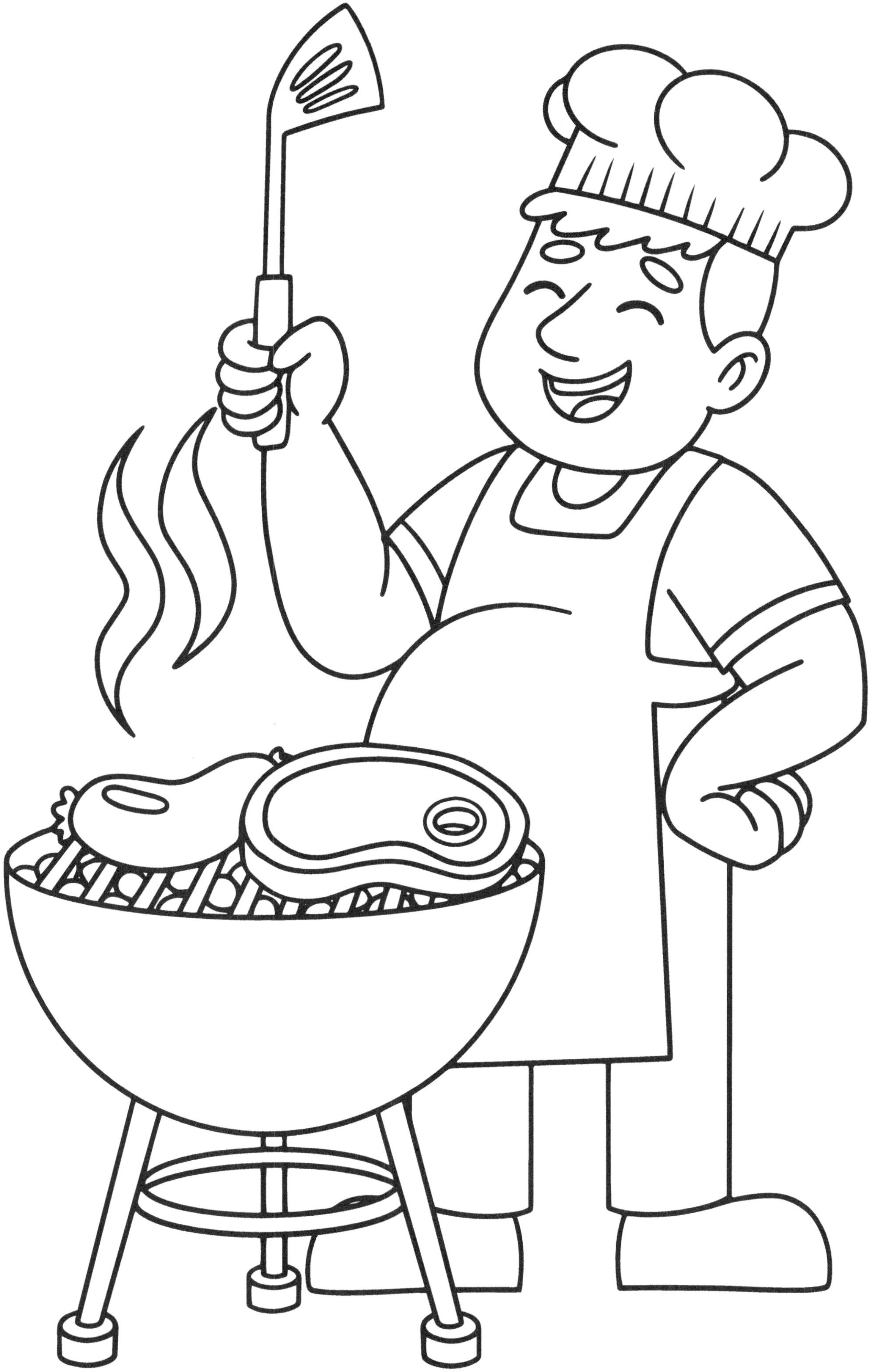

COOKIES!

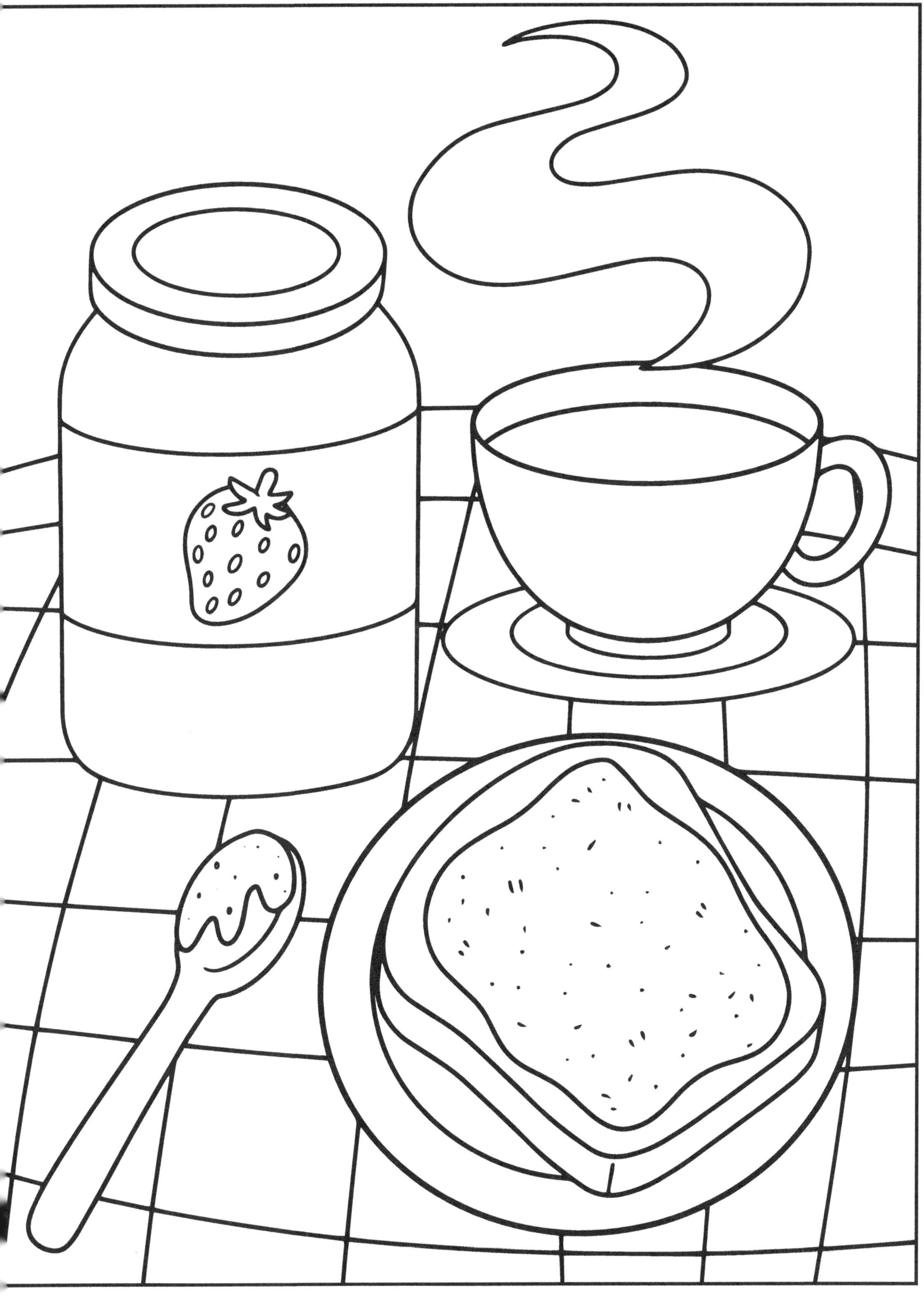

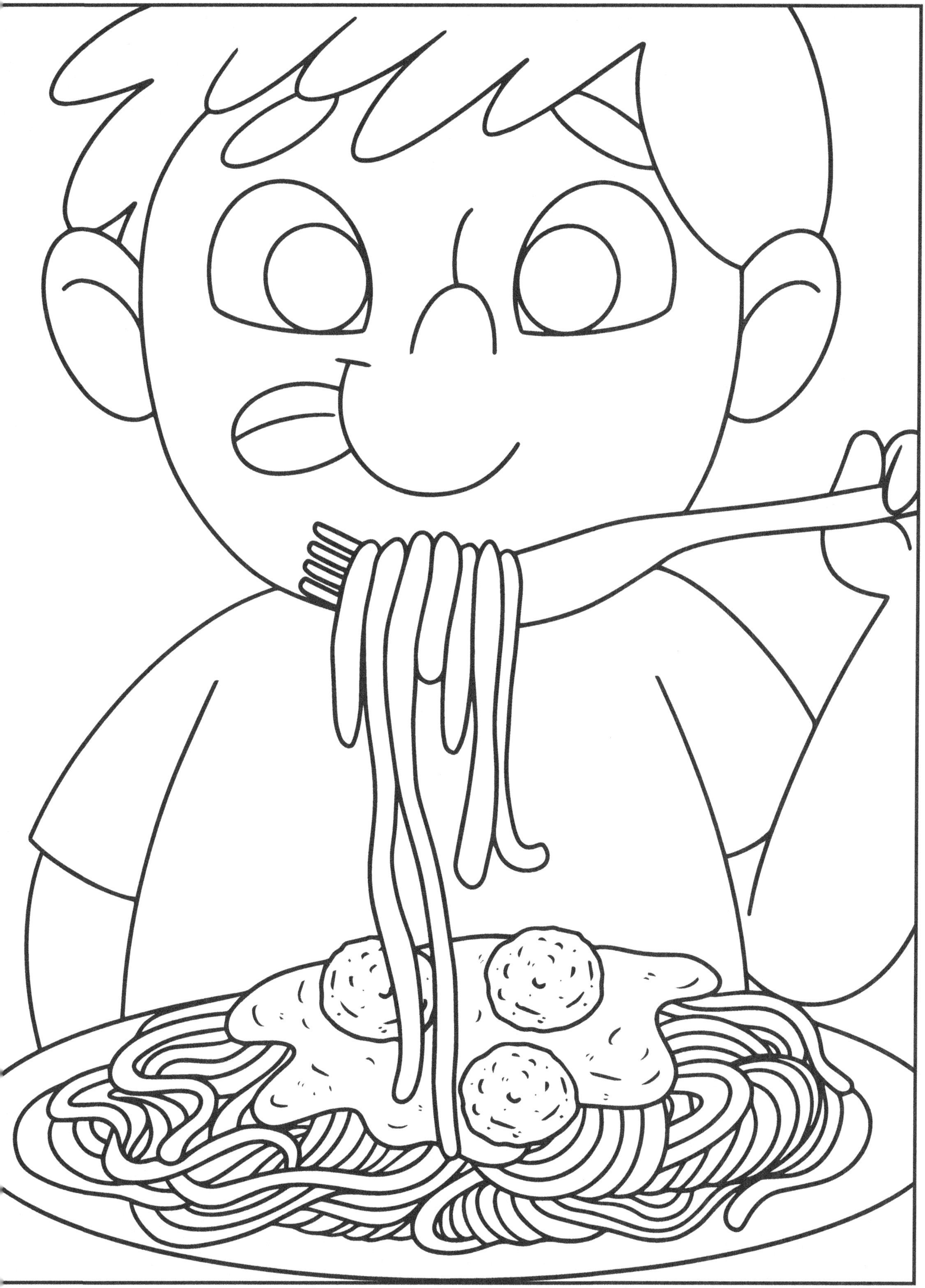

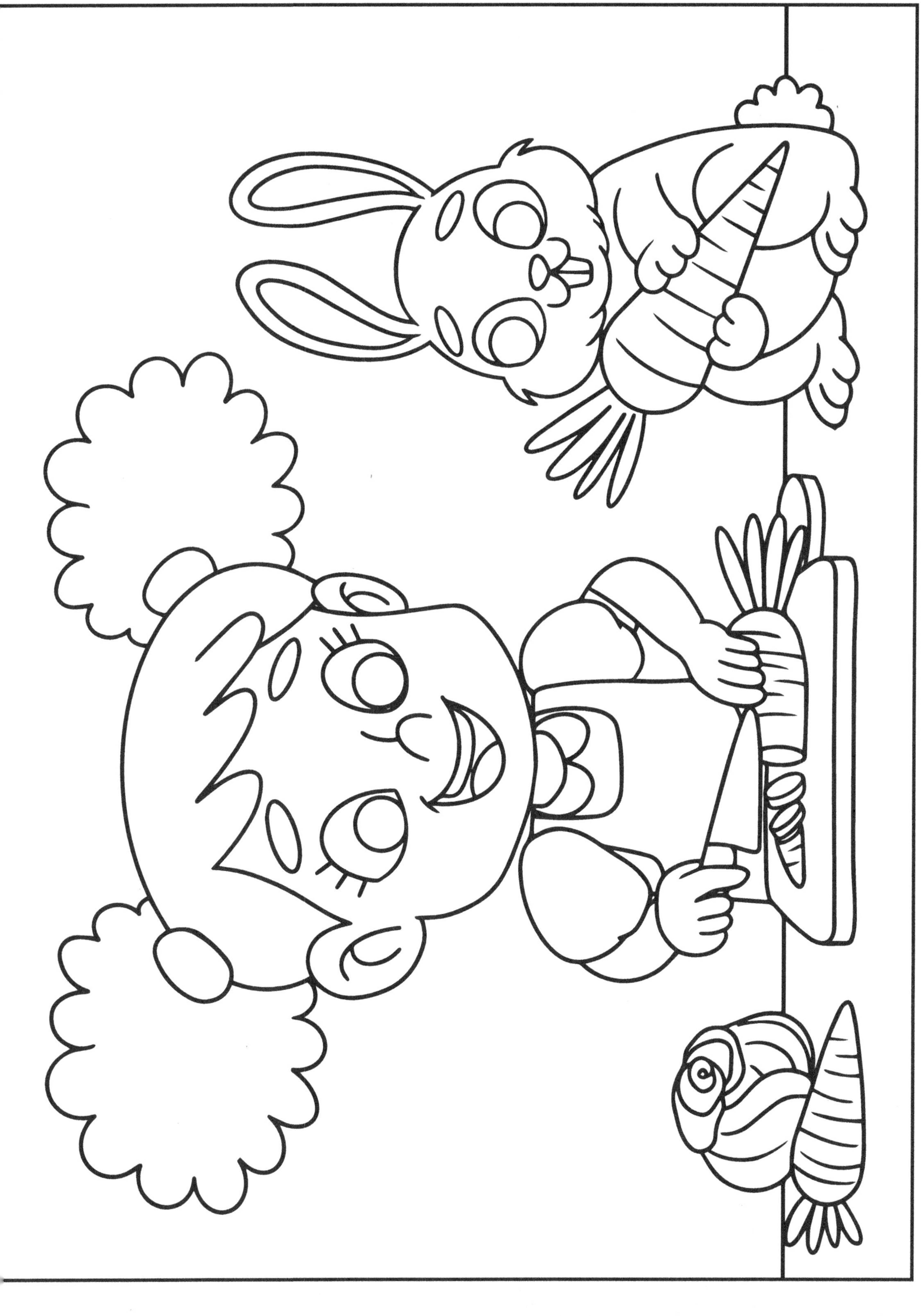

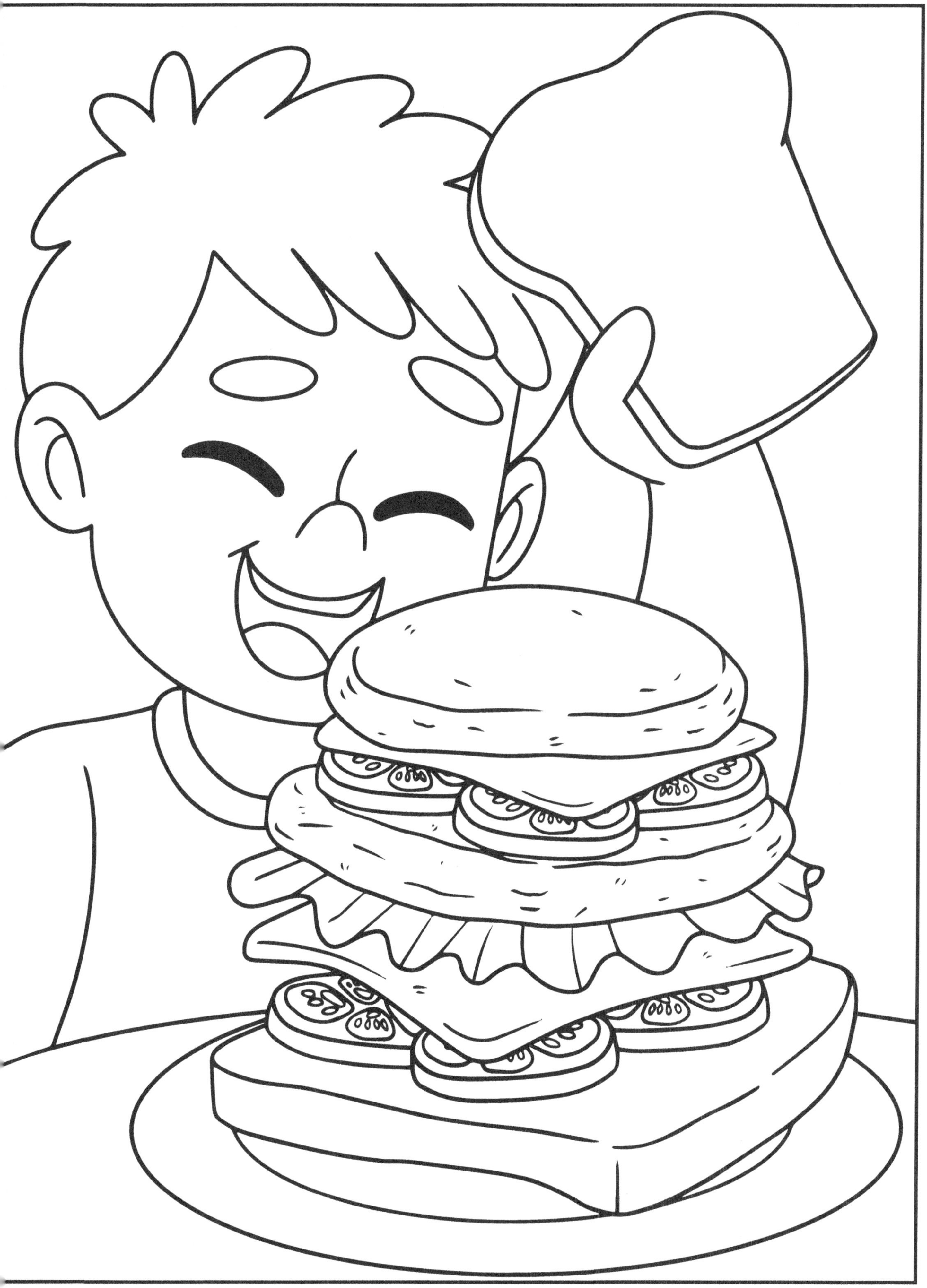

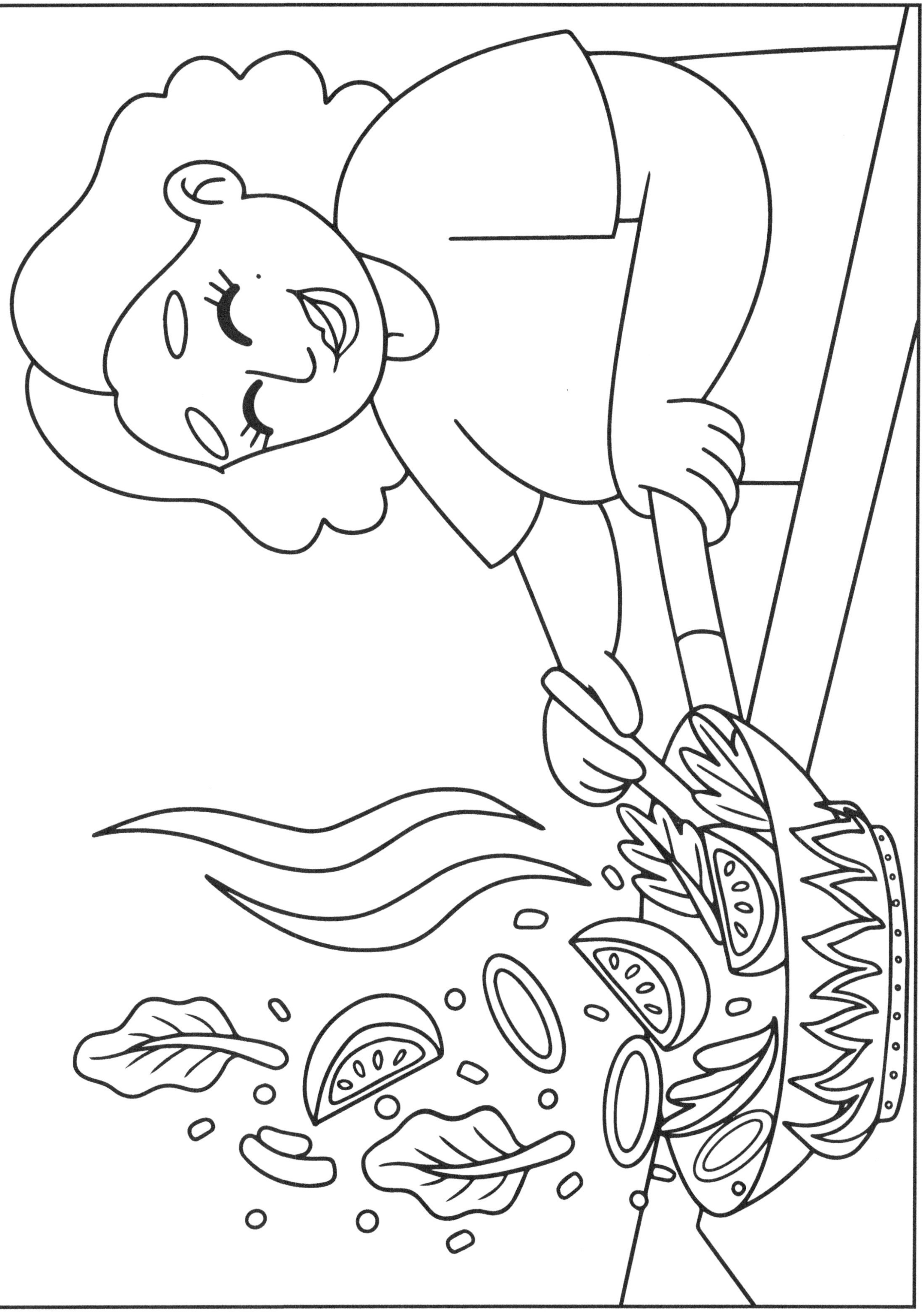

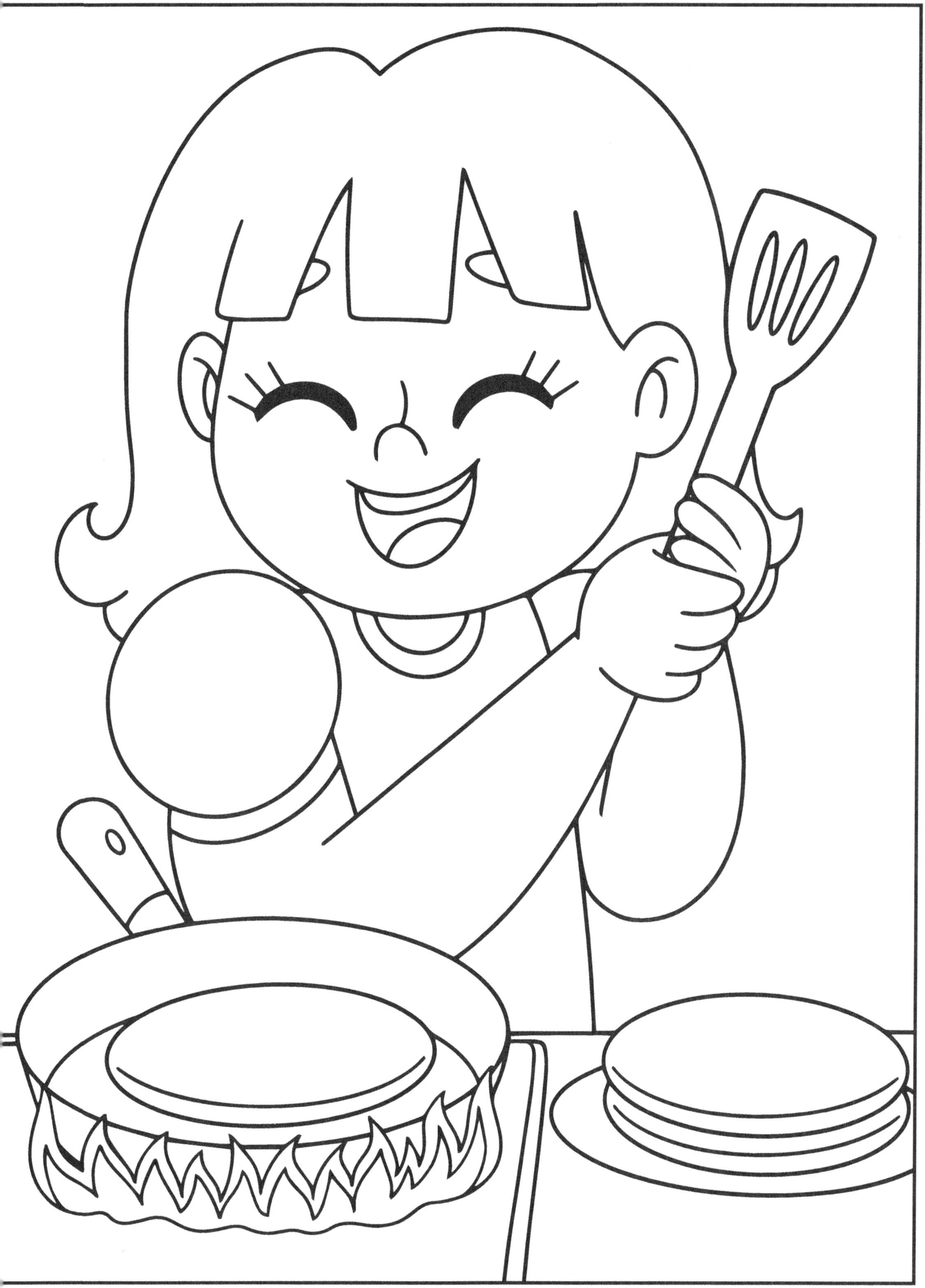

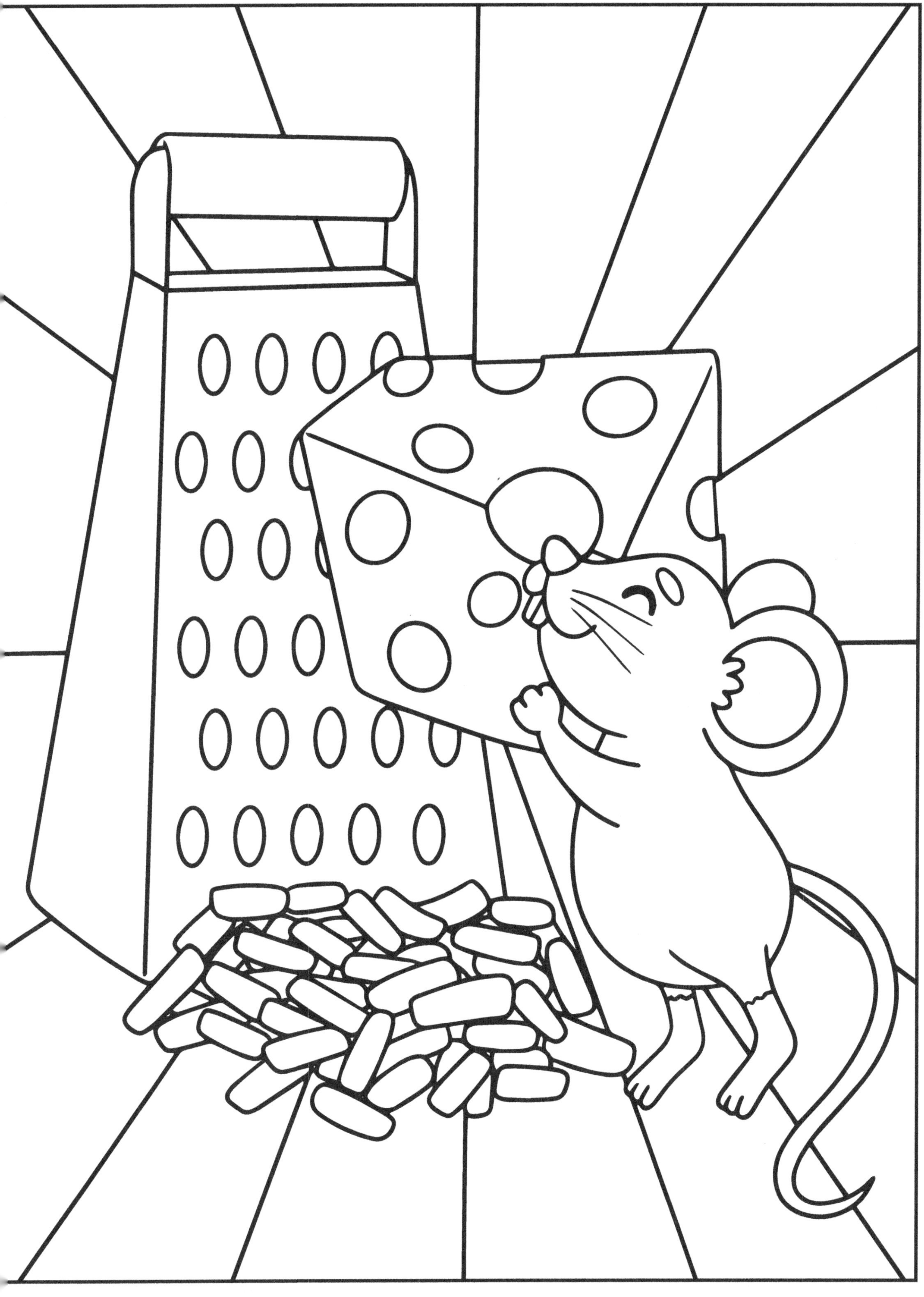

SUGAR

Made in the USA
Coppell, TX
08 April 2025